THE KINGDOM & LEGACY BUILDER
Dr. Renee Sunday, M.D.

Business
& *Blessed*

*A Faith-Based Framework for
Unshakable Business Growth*

Copyright © 2025 – All rights reserved.

No part of this publication may be reproduced, distributed, or transmitted in any form or by any means, including photocopying, recording, or other electronic or mechanical methods, without the prior written permission of the publisher, except in the case of brief quotations embodied in critical reviews and certain other noncommercial uses permitted by copyright law.

Table of Contents

I. A Note from Dr. Renee Sunday	6
II. Introduction: The Faith-Fueled Path to Business Resilience	9
III. The 12 Business & Blessed Action Steps	12

Kingdom Key 1: Embrace Your Kingdom Assignment
Kingdom Key 2: Build on the Rock – Foundational Clarity
Kingdom Key 3: Develop Spirit-Led Systems
Kingdom Key 4: Protect Your Peace (and Your Energy)
Kingdom Key 5: Master Consistency Over Chaos
Kingdom Key 6: Know Your Value & Charge Accordingly
Kingdom Key 7: Create Crisis-Proof Revenue Streams
Kingdom Key 8: Surround Yourself with Faith-Fueled Support
Kingdom Key 9: Keep the Vision Before You
Kingdom Key 10: Align Your Schedule with God's Pace
Kingdom Key 11: Use Feedback as Fuel
Kingdom Key 12: Trust God with the Results

IV. Reflection Journal & Guided Prompts	88
V. Next Steps: Your Strategy Session Invitation	114
VI. About Dr. Renee Sunday	122

A Note from Dr. Renee Sunday, MD

My Beloved Kingdom Entrepreneur,

It is no accident that you're holding this book. I believe in divine timing, and I believe in you. You were chosen *for such a time as this*—to rise, to build, to lead, and to serve with power and purpose.

As a physician, minister, media mogul, and business strategist, I've seen the power of combining marketplace impact with spiritual alignment. Let me tell you: when you let God be your CEO, everything changes. Your vision sharpens. Your courage deepens. And your results—oh, they multiply.

Business & Blessed is not just another business manual. It's a prophetic blueprint. A faith-based framework born from real battles, bold prayers, and breakthrough after breakthrough. In these pages, you'll find not just information, but impartation. You'll learn how to anchor your business in biblical principles while executing with marketplace excellence.

So I challenge you, right now: lean in. Take notes. Pray. Reflect. Apply. Let the Holy Spirit lead you into strategy, into stewardship, and into success that doesn't just make noise—it makes legacy.

You are not just building a business. You are advancing the Kingdom. You are breaking generational chains. You are answering a divine call.

A NOTE FROM DR. RENEE SUNDAY, MD

Let's walk this journey together. I'm cheering you on every step of the way.

In faith and fullness,

Dr. Renee Sunday, MD
Media Personality | Business Strategist | Marketplace Minister

INTRODUCTION

The Faith-Fueled Path to Business Resilience

*Your Business is Not Just a Vision—
It's a Vessel for God's Glory*

M y dear Kingdom CEO,

Let me prophesy to your potential for a moment: You were never meant to play small. You were never meant to chase success the world's way. You were created to dominate in your assignment—with clarity, authority, and divine strategy. That's what this journey is about.

When I began building in business, media, and ministry, I quickly discovered talent isn't enough. Degrees aren't enough. Even good intentions aren't enough. What sustains and

INTRODUCTION

elevates a business—especially in uncertain times—is a foundation rooted in faith. Not just faith in yourself, but faith in the One who called you.

That's why Business & Blessed was birthed—not just out of experience, but out of obedience. This isn't theory. This is revelation. It's wisdom sharpened by warfare, strategies refined through seasons of struggle, and anointing pressed from obedience in private.

This book will show you how to:

- 🔒 Anchor your business in the Word without losing your edge in the world

- 🔒 Align your systems with divine order, not just trends

- 🔒 Cultivate resilience that's not reactive, but rooted

- 🔒 Operate with boldness, clarity, and supernatural expectation

INTRODUCTION

You won't just read this book—you'll activate it. Each page is designed to pour into your spirit, stretch your mindset, and expand your capacity. Because I'm not just talking to your today—I'm speaking to the version of you who's already walking in overflow, impact, and divine alignment.

Let me tell you this: The world needs what God placed in you. Your voice, your business, your brilliance—it's all Kingdom currency. It's time to stop second-guessing and start building like the heir you are.

So take a deep breath. Say a prayer. And turn the page. Because everything you've been praying for? It starts right here.

In power and purpose,
Dr. Renee Sunday, MD
Marketplace Mentor | CEO Mentor | Midwife to Destiny

12 Business & Blessed

ACTION STEPS

KINGDOM KEY 01

Embrace Your Kingdom Assignment

"Before I formed you in the womb I knew you, before you were born I set you apart."
– JEREMIAH 1:5

Before there was a logo, a business plan, or a vision board—there was **God's calling on your life**. He knew exactly what He was doing when He gave you that business idea. It wasn't random. It was a Kingdom assignment placed in your spirit to bless others and glorify Him.

Many entrepreneurs chase trends or hustle endlessly for success... but *Kingdom entrepreneurs* build differently. We build from identity, not insecurity. From obedience, not pressure. And from clarity, not chaos.

EMBRACE YOUR KINGDOM ASSIGNMENT

Your business is **not separate from your ministry**—it *is* your ministry. Whether you're coaching, creating, consulting, or crafting, God wants to use your skills, experience, and story to **bring light into dark places**.

Many faith-based entrepreneurs wrestle with imposter syndrome, thinking, "Who am I to lead?" or "What if I get it wrong?" But when you're on assignment from God, your authority doesn't come from your résumé—it comes from your yes. Heaven is not looking for perfect resumes; it's looking for obedient vessels.

Your story, your scars, your skills—they all qualify you to lead with authenticity and compassion.

The enemy's tactic is always the same: **confuse your identity, distract your focus, and discourage your heart.** That's why it's critical that you anchor your business in God's voice, not just industry noise. When you know you're operating under a Kingdom mandate, **you won't**

panic in hard seasons, because you understand you're backed by Heaven, not hustling on your own.

Your assignment isn't just about profits—it's about **people**. Real souls are on the other side of your obedience. The breakthrough you've experienced, the wisdom you've gained, the solutions you've developed—they're all seeds meant to multiply in the lives of others. This is how we turn a business into a *Kingdom engine*—not just producing wealth, but reproducing impact.

Lastly, embracing your Kingdom assignment means you **walk in daily partnership with the Holy Spirit**. Not just in worship or prayer, but in planning, pitching, launching, serving, hiring, and leading. You're not a solo CEO—you're co-laboring with the Creator of the universe. There is no greater business partner than God Himself.

Too many believers treat business like a side hustle to their faith instead of a **sacred space to**

EMBRACE YOUR KINGDOM ASSIGNMENT

express their faith. But you were called to show up in the marketplace as a light—not to shrink, blend in, or water down your assignment to make others comfortable. When you embrace your Kingdom identity, you stop apologizing for being bold, Spirit-led, and unapologetically faith-filled in how you build and serve.

This kind of boldness doesn't come from motivational quotes—it comes from intimacy with God. The more you commune with Him, the more clarity you receive about why you've been positioned in this season, with these people, for this purpose.

This isn't about doing more. It's about **doing what matters most**—and doing it with God, not just for Him.

You also need to know: You are the answer to someone's prayer. Someone is right now crying out for clarity, healing, breakthrough, or transformation—and the solution is inside your story, your products, your obedience. When you don't embrace your assignment, those people keep waiting. But when you say yes, lives shift.

And finally, embracing your assignment doesn't mean you'll always feel ready—it means you trust that God is. Every yes you give Him becomes a door He opens. Every time you show up in faith, He shows out in favor. You don't have to have it all figured out—just walk with the One who does.

Faith-Fueled Action Steps:

1. PRAY BOLDLY

Ask: "Holy Spirit, show me where You want to use my business to serve Your people."

2. WRITE YOUR BUSINESS CALLING STATEMENT.

One to two sentences that reflect your God-given purpose in the marketplace.

3. COMMIT TO KINGDOM-LED LEADERSHIP

Every decision, every offer, every launch—submit it in prayer first.

EMBRACE YOUR KINGDOM ASSIGNMENT

Journal Prompts:

🔒 What burdens do I carry for others that could be solved through my business?

_____
_____
_____
_____

🔒 Where has God already opened doors that confirm this is my lane?

_____
_____
_____
_____

🔒 How can I start showing up more boldly as a Kingdom leader in my niche?

_____
_____
_____
_____

KINGDOM KEY 02

Build on the Rock
Foundational Clarity

"Therefore everyone who hears these words of mine and puts them into practice is like a wise man who built his house on the rock."

– MATTHEW 7:24

In business, storms are not a matter of if—they're a matter of when. The question is: what are you building on? Too many entrepreneurs build their business on shifting trends, emotional highs, or hustler culture—and when adversity hits, everything collapses.

But Kingdom entrepreneurs build on **the Rock**.

BUILD ON THE ROCK FOUNDATIONAL CLARITY

That Rock is **Christ, His Word, and His wisdom.**

He is not just the God of your salvation—He wants to be the **CEO of your strategy.**

Before you can scale your business, you must **solidify your foundation**. That means answering some hard but holy questions:

- Who is your business really serving?
- What is your God-given solution to their problem?
- Why does your offer matter in the Kingdom?

When your business foundation is rooted in clarity, not confusion—you'll stop pivoting out of panic and start operating from divine precision.

A strong foundation in business isn't just structural—**it's spiritual**. That means spending time in God's presence before rushing into performance. When you build on the Rock, your first team meeting each week is with the Holy

Spirit. Your boardroom becomes a prayer room. And clarity doesn't come from guesswork—it comes from *revelation*.

God is strategic. He didn't create the world in chaos; He used order, sequence, and vision. In the same way, your business needs structure that supports the vision—not stifles it. When you're constantly starting over, changing directions, or copying others, it's often a sign that your foundation is shaky.

But when you're anchored in divine clarity, your **confidence increases, your messaging sharpens, and your results multiply.**

Clarity also attracts clients. People are drawn to leaders who know exactly who they are, who they serve, and what transformation they offer. When you're rooted in your Kingdom identity and purpose, **your voice carries authority**—not just charisma. This makes your marketing feel more like ministry and your content feel more like calling.

BUILD ON THE ROCK FOUNDATIONAL CLARITY

Finally, let this be your reminder: clarity is not a one-time download—it's a rhythm. As your business evolves, your clarity must deepen. That means revisiting your foundation regularly in prayer and strategy sessions with God.

Let Him recalibrate your heart, reveal blind spots, and affirm the direction He's given you.

Clarity-Building Action Steps:

1. **CLARIFY YOU CALLING IN ONE SENTENCE.**
   Ask: "Holy Spirit, show me where You want to use my business to serve Your people."

2. **OUTLINE YOUR CORE VALUES.**
   What principles are non-negotiable in your brand and business decisions?

3. **AUDIT YOUR OFFER.**
   Is it still in alignment with the problem God has anointed you to solve?

Journal Prompts:

- Am I building based on what's popular—or what God said?

- What would change if I fully submitted my business model to God?

- Where have I allowed confusion or busyness to cover up what God made clear?

KINGDOM KEY 03

Develop Spirit-Led Systems

"Let all things be done decently and in order."
— 1 CORINTHIANS 14:40

Systems may sound like the least spiritual part of your business, but they are actually one of the most sacred. Why? Because God is a God of order, and systems are how we bring divine order into our day-to-day operations.

Chaos is not Kingdom.

Burnout is not biblical.
And being overwhelmed is not proof that you're

DEVELOP SPIRIT-LED SYSTEMS

doing enough—it's often proof that your systems need a supernatural upgrade.

If you're spending more time putting out fires than planting seeds, it's time to invite the Holy Spirit into your structure. Systems aren't meant to suffocate your creativity or spontaneity—they're meant to **protect your peace and multiply your impact.**

Spirit-led systems are not rigid. They are **rooted in wisdom and revelation.** They allow you to serve more people, steward your time better, and make room for rest. They help you say "yes" to the right things—and confidently say "no" to distractions. Every Kingdom entrepreneur needs systems to support their God-given assignment, so you can focus on vision, not just execution.

One of the biggest lies in business is that working harder equals greater impact. But the truth is, **working smarter through divine structure brings lasting fruit.** Think of Jesus feeding the 5,000—He told the disciples to organize the people into groups before the miracle multiplied. The structure preceded the overflow.

If you're constantly chasing your to-do list or living in reactive mode, you don't need more motivation—you need alignment. It's time to stop building on broken workflows and start building Spirit-led systems that reflect how God wants you to operate, in this season, with your unique grace.

Spirit-led systems start with asking: "What has God actually called me to do—and how can I do it with excellence and peace?" From your daily schedule to your email flow, everything should flow from the grace God has given you, not the pressure of trying to keep up with worldly pace. Your systems should serve you—not enslave you.

When you design your business systems around your spiritual rhythm, everything shifts. You'll notice you're less reactive and more responsive. Less overwhelmed and more focused. Systems give you the ability to scale your assignment

DEVELOP SPIRIT-LED SYSTEMS

without compromising your health, family, or walk with God. They allow you to lead, not just survive.

It might look like automating onboarding, setting time-blocks for focused work, delegating what drains you, or building out your client journey with clarity. But the point isn't to copy someone else's setup. It's to build the infrastructure that matches your Kingdom identity, mission, and capacity.

And here's the secret: Spirit-led systems leave room for miracles. When God wants to accelerate your growth or send divine connections, your systems are what catch the overflow. Without systems, increase can become stressful. With systems, it becomes sustainable. You're no longer managing chaos—you're **hosting Kingdom flow.**

Spirit-Led System Action Steps:

1. **AUDIT YOUR OPERATIONS**
   What areas of your business feel chaotic or draining?

2. **PRIORITIZE PEACE**
   Identify one system to simplify this week (e.g. client onboarding, scheduling, social media).

3. **PRAY FOR DIVINE STRUCTURE**
   Ask the Holy Spirit to show you the systems that suit your calling—not just your goals.

Journal Prompts:

What area of my business would operate smoother with a better systems?

_____
_____
_____
_____

DEVELOP SPIRIT-LED SYSTEMS

🔒 Where am I over-functioning in my business due to a lack of structure?

_____

_____

_____

_____

_____

_____

🔒 What is God calling me to let go of, automate, or delegate?

_____

_____

_____

_____

_____

_____

KINGDOM KEY 04

Protect Your Peace (and Energy)

"Peace I leave with you; my peace I give you. I do not give to you as the world gives. Do not let your hearts be troubled and do not be afraid."
– JOHN 14:27

In the Kingdom, peace is not a luxury—it's a strategy. It's your spiritual weapon, your leadership posture, and your secret advantage.

You were never called to build a business out of burnout, exhaustion, or emotional chaos. As a faith-based entrepreneur, your greatest asset is not your productivity—it's your peace. When you lead from a place of overflow, not overwork, you reflect the pace and power of Heaven.

Peace is a **byproduct of alignment**. If your spirit is overwhelmed, it often means you're carrying something God didn't assign to you. And if your calendar is full but your heart is frustrated, it might be time to surrender your "yes" back to the Lord. God is not impressed with busy builders. He's moved by obedient ones.

Protecting your peace also means setting **healthy boundaries**—spiritually, relationally, mentally, and energetically. That includes saying no without guilt, creating Sabbath rhythms, and honoring your capacity. When you say "yes" to everyone, you dilute your "yes" to God.

You are not called to be everything to everyone. Jesus had boundaries. He walked away from crowds. He went off to pray. He rested—even in the middle of storms. If the Son of God modeled margin, so should you. **Peace is the fruit of boundaries.**

Sometimes peace isn't lost—it's **leaked**. Through constant notifications. Through late-night overthinking. Through trying to fix things God never told you to control. You must begin to **protect your mental and spiritual energy with intentionality**. That means auditing your inputs: What are you watching? Listening to? Speaking over yourself?

Peace is a **position of trust**. When you're truly surrendered to God's pace, you stop letting urgency drive you and start letting discernment lead you. That doesn't mean you won't have deadlines or challenges—but it means you don't face them alone, and you don't let them disrupt your inner stillness. You carry peace not because of your situation, but because of your **Source**.

When you prioritize your peace, you'll start to notice something shift in your business: **divine clarity becomes easier, creativity flows more freely, and decisions become simpler**. Why? Because peace tunes your spiritual ears. It helps you hear God's voice without all the static of stress. That's why the enemy fights your peace—

PROTECT YOUR PEACE (AND ENERGY)

because when you're calm, you're *dangerous*.

Your energy is sacred. You are not a machine. You are a vessel—chosen, anointed, and human. That means your energy needs **restoration, not depletion**. Protecting your energy looks like starting your day in prayer, giving yourself margin, and refusing to hustle for validation. It's choosing alignment over activity and wisdom over weariness.

Here's your permission slip: You don't have to prove your worth through productivity. God already approved you. He's not waiting for you to "do more"—He's calling you to **be with Him more**, and let that intimacy fuel every move you make.

Peace & Energy Action Steps:

1. **AUDIT YOUR INPUTS**
   What drains you emotionally, spiritually, or physically? Begin eliminating or adjusting it.

CREATE MARGIN
Block out intentional time this week for rest, reflection, and realignment with God.

SET A PEACE PLAN
What habits will you commit to that restore your peace daily (e.g. prayer walks, boundaries, digital detox)?

Journal Prompts:

Where have I allowed busyness to replace intimacy with God?

_____
_____
_____
_____
_____
_____
_____
_____

PROTECT YOUR PEACE (AND ENERGY)

🔒 What boundaries do I need to set or strengthen to protect my peace?

_____

_____

_____

_____

_____

🔒 What does peace feel like to me—and how can I prioritize that feeling in business?

_____

_____

_____

_____

_____

KINGDOM KEY 05

Master Consistency Over Chaos

"Let us not become weary in doing good, for at the proper time we will reap a harvest if we do not give up."

– GALATIANS 6:9

Consistency is where the miracles manifest.

Not in the grand gestures. Not in the viral posts. Not in the "hustle hard" hype.

But in the daily decisions to **show up, obey, and build—brick by brick.**

MASTER CONSISTENCY OVER CHAOS

The world rewards speed, but the Kingdom honors **steadfastness.** God is not looking for trendy leaders—He's looking for faithful ones. The enemy of your harvest isn't just laziness—it's inconsistency. Chaos creeps in every time discipline breaks down. But when you master the rhythm of consistency, you create momentum that Heaven can multiply.

Being consistent doesn't mean doing the most. It means doing the right things repeatedly, even when they feel unseen, unpopular, or uncelebrated. Showing up to serve that one client well. Sending the email no one responded to last time. Praying over your business when it feels dry. **These acts of obedience build legacy.**

And here's the secret: **God multiplies what you maintain.** He's not asking you to be perfect. He's asking you to be planted. There's power in rootedness. There's breakthrough in staying the course. Your consistency becomes a spiritual weapon—silencing the lies of doubt, dismantling distractions, and pulling future fruit into your now season.

Inconsistent action often comes from unclear identity. If you're constantly stopping, starting, or shifting directions, it's time to reconnect with why you started. Go back to the last clear word God gave you. Were you called to this? If yes, then don't let temporary resistance make you abandon your permanent assignment.

Consistency requires **covenant thinking**. It's understanding that you're not just building for today's results—you're building in response to God's assignment. When you see your business as a covenant with Heaven, *faithfulness becomes your strategy*. You stop chasing quick wins and start investing in *eternal fruit*.

You don't have to feel motivated to be consistent —you need to be *anchored*. Anchored in your calling. Anchored in your "why." Anchored in your agreement with God. Motivation fades, but commitment to purpose keeps you steady even when emotions shift.

Chaos thrives in the absence of systems,

MASTER CONSISTENCY OVER CHAOS

structure, and spiritual discipline. And let's be honest: for many of us, inconsistency is a result of **emotional leadership**. We move when we feel like it, and we stop when it gets hard. But Kingdom entrepreneurs lead with *conviction*, not convenience.

God blesses what we are faithful with. He's a rewarder of those who diligently seek Him—not occasionally, not when it's trendy, but diligently. If you want to see overflow, fruit, and fulfillment—you need to **outlast the noise** with your quiet, consistent yes.

You must treat your calling like it's already fruitful, even when you don't see results yet. Because faith doesn't wait for confirmation—it **creates** it. Show up for your business the way you expect clients to show up for you: consistently, with excellence, and with belief in the outcome.

And finally, give yourself grace. Consistency doesn't mean perfection—it means progress. If you miss a day, get back up. If you drop the ball, reset. But whatever you do, don't quit. Your consistency is a seed—and God is the God of the harvest.

Consistency Activation Steps:

1. PICK YOUR 3 NON-NEGOTIABLES
What 3 business habits will you commit to daily or weekly?

2. CREATE A WEEKLY CHECK-IN WITH GOD
Use this time to review, reflect, and recalibrate.

3. SET A FAITHFUL FOCUS TRACKER
Track how often you complete key tasks, not for guilt—but for growth.

Journal Prompts:

- Where in my business do I struggle with consistency the most—and why?

- What does faithfulness look like for me in this season?

- How can I structure my week to reflect my commitment to the vision God gave me?

KINGDOM KEY 06

Know Your Value & Charge Accordingly

"A worker deserves his wages."

– LUKE 10:7

There is nothing humble about undercharging when you're carrying Heaven's solution.

You are not doing the world a favor by playing small, shrinking your value, or giving your services away out of guilt.

As a Kingdom entrepreneur, your pricing should reflect **not only your skill—but your impact.**

It's time to dismantle the belief that money and ministry can't mix. You are not selling salvation—you are stewarding a business that solves problems, transforms lives, and sustains your assignment.

God has called you to **serve people with integrity and excellence**—but He's also called you to **build something sustainable**. Your business is not just a blessing to others, it's supposed to be a blessing to you and your household. Charging your worth is not selfish. It's **stewardship**.

When you discount your services to please people or avoid rejection, you train your audience to **devalue your anointing**. You're not just a coach, consultant, or creative—you're a Kingdom solution-carrier. There's a divine deposit inside of you, and that deserves honor—including financially.

The truth is, most pricing issues are actually **identity issues**. When you don't fully own your value, it shows up in what you charge, how you pitch, and how confidently you sell. But when you see yourself as God sees you—a trusted leader equipped for impact—you price, present, and position yourself accordingly.

The enemy wants you to stay small so you won't fully fund your assignment.

If he can keep you undercharging, he can keep you **overworking and under-resourced**. But Kingdom entrepreneurs aren't meant to scrape by—we're called to **build with overflow**. That means pricing with intention, clarity, and courage.

Jesus didn't operate in lack. He multiplied what was in His hands. You are not an expense to your clients—you are an investment. And when you price properly, you give others the opportunity to honor what God placed in you.

Discounting from fear is very different from

serving from generosity. There are moments to give, sow, or gift—but that should come from *discernment*, not desperation. Don't allow people-pleasing or imposter syndrome to rob your revenue. Remember, **your pricing is prophetic**. It tells the world how you see yourself and what you believe your impact is worth.

You may be called to fund missions, build legacy, hire help, create resources, or bless others—but how can you do that if you're stuck charging less than your grace carries? It's time to release the fear of being "too expensive" and step into **divine alignment with what your work is truly worth.**

Want practical proof? Think about this: your ideal client is waiting for someone to lead them with confidence. When you undercharge, you often attract the wrong clients—those who don't value transformation, waste your time, or don't follow through. **Aligned pricing creates aligned partnerships.**

Also, remember: value isn't just in your deliverables—it's in your presence, your perspective, your wisdom, and your walk. You carry a history with God. You've overcomebattles. You've gained revelation. That is not cheap. Don't make others pay less for what it cost *you everything to carry.*

And lastly, this: you are allowed to profit and prosper. There's nothing holy about poverty. The Proverbs 31 woman was a businesswoman. Paul was a tentmaker. Jesus had a treasurer. **Financial fruit funds Kingdom influence.** The more you grow, the more you can give. The more you charge, the more margin you have to serve from rest, not resentment.

Peace & Energy Action Steps:

1. AUDIT YOUR OFFERS
Are your prices reflecting your transformation, experience, and impact?

REFRAME YOUR PRICING MINDSET

Replace fear-based thoughts with faith-based truths about money and worth.

DECLARE YOUR WORTH DAILY

Speak life over your business: "I charge with confidence, I serve with excellence, and I attract aligned clients."

Journal Prompts:

Where have I been undercharging due to fear or people-pleasing?

_____
_____
_____
_____
_____
_____
_____
_____

KNOW YOUR VALUE & CHARGE ACCORDINGLY

🔒 What would change if I fully owned my value as a Kingdom entrepreneur?

_____
_____
_____
_____
_____
_____
_____

🔒 How does God want me to price in a way that honors both my mission and my margin?

_____
_____
_____
_____
_____
_____
_____
_____

KINGDOM KEY 07

Create Crisis-Proof Revenue Streams

"Give portions to seven, yes to eight, for you do not know what disaster may come upon the land."

– ECCLESIASTES 11:2 (NIV)

If the last few years taught us anything, it's this: one stream is not enough.

The world is unstable. Markets shift. Clients pause. Platforms change. But *you*—as a Kingdom builder—must remain steady, positioned, and **prepared**.

God is calling faith-based entrepreneurs to **build**

CREATE CRISIS-PROOF REVENUE STREAMS

businesses that thrive in every season, not just in times of ease. That requires more than vision. It requires **diversified, durable, and Spirit-led revenue.** Crisis-proof revenue streams don't just protect your finances—they protect your assignment.

This doesn't mean hustling to create 20 different offers. It means being strategic with the wisdom of Heaven. It means asking, "Lord, how can I package what You've placed in me in multiple ways so it can serve more people, in more places, at any time?"

God gave you more than one gift. So why settle for one stream?

Jesus didn't just preach—He taught, healed, mentored, and multiplied. Likewise, you can generate income through multiple channels: coaching, courses, digital products, speaking, memberships, licensing, books, brand partnerships—and more. Every skill, testimony, tool, and transformation you carry is *potential income when stewarded with faith and strategy.*

The enemy would love for you to stay in survival mode—barely making it, always reacting, and never building margin. But God's plan is **overflow, not instability**. That means building with the future in mind. That means stewarding now *for what's next.*

When you diversify your income streams under divine direction, you create **space for God to multiply**. You move from praying for provision to *partnering with it*. Not only that, but you build capacity to continue your mission—even when one area slows down.

Don't wait until a crisis forces you to pivot—**build now**. Ask the Lord to reveal which streams align with your current season, your bandwidth, and your audience. You're not called to do *everything*, but you are called to steward multiple *expressions* of the gift He's given you.

CREATE CRISIS-PROOF REVENUE STREAMS

Start with what's in your hand. You already have something you've created, solved, or spoken that could be repurposed into a new stream. Maybe it's a workshop that becomes a digital course. A one-on-one service that becomes a group program. A journal entry that becomes a devotional. **God multiplies what you release.**

Also, remember: crisis-proof revenue is **not just about survival—it's about Kingdom expansion.** It allows you to give more, hire more, reach more, and serve without fear. It gives you the freedom to say "yes" to divine assignments that don't come with a paycheck—but come with purpose.

Building multiple streams also protects your peace. When one offer is slow, you're not panicking—you're pivoting. When one audience isn't responding, you're not paralyzed—you have options. This is how Kingdom entrepreneurs lead with confidence in uncertain times.

It's not unspiritual to plan for profit. **It's unwise**

not to. The Proverbs 31 woman "considered afield and bought it." Joseph stored in seasons of plenty. Jesus told parables about investments. You are not called to wait passively—you are called to **build proactively.**

And here's the key: not all streams will be loud. Some will be evergreen, automated, or hidden behind the scenes—but they'll flow because you obeyed. Some will take time. Some will take trial. But each one, birthed in faith, **will sustain your vision long term.**

Multiple Stream Action Steps:

1. **INVENTORY YOUR GIFTS & OFFERS**
   What 3 business habits will you commit to daily or weekly?

2. **PRAY FOR STRATEGY**
   Ask God to reveal 1-2 revenue ideas He wants you to activate next.

3. **CREATE ONE STREAM THIS MONTH**
   Start small. Test it. Refine it. But start.

Journal Prompts:

🔒 What mindset or fear has stopped me from building more than one stream?

_____
_____
_____
_____
_____

🔒 What is already in my hand that God wants to multiply?

_____
_____
_____
_____
_____

🔒 What would a business look like that operates well—even during a storm?

_____
_____
_____
_____

KINGDOM KEY 08

Surround Yourself with Faith-Fueled Support

Two are better than one... If either of them falls down, one can help the other up."

– ECCLESIASTES 4:9-10

You weren't designed to build your business in isolation. Even Jesus had 12. Paul had Barnabas. Moses had Aaron David had Jonathan.

Every visionary needs **faith-filled voices, not just followers.**

You need people who see your calling, speak life into your process, and stand with you in the

SURROUND YOURSELF WITH FAITH-FUELED SUPPORT

trenches. Your business can't thrive if your support system is starving—or worse, *toxic.*

This isn't just about networking. This is about **Kingdom alignment.**

Who is helping you war in prayer? Who is holding you accountable when you're tired or drifting off course? Who's reminding you of what God said when your emotions start speaking louder than your faith?

> The wrong circle will pressure you to perform.
> The right circle will push you to pray.
> The wrong crowd will water down your fire.
> The right community will fan it into flame.

Isolation is a tactic of the enemy. If he can get you alone, discouraged, and disconnected, he can start whispering lies: *"You're the only one struggling... no one understands... maybe you're not really called..."* But when you're surrounded by **faith-fueled voices**, those lies lose their power.

A faith-filled support system isn't just about emotional comfort—it's about **spiritual protection.** When you're surrounded by people who hear God, speak truth, and walk in alignment, your business becomes **battle-proofed.** You gain wisdom, intercession, and strategy—not just encouragement.

Not everyone deserves a front-row seat to your vision.

Some people are spectators. Some are siphons. Some are sent by God to **speak life and hold your arms up like Aaron and Hur did for Moses.** You must be discerning about who's speaking into your business—and your identity.

Faith-fueled support also includes **mentorship and accountability.** You don't grow in the dark. You grow in the light—through conversations, challenges, and coaching that stretch your thinking and sharpen your calling. You were never meant to figure everything out alone. God uses *people* to unlock your next level.

SURROUND YOURSELF WITH FAITH-FUELED SUPPORT

And let's be real: entrepreneurship can be lonely. Especially when you're walking with integrity in industries that glorify ego, compromise, and performance. That's why **Kingdom community is your lifeline.** It reminds you: You're not crazy. You're *called.*

You need support that doesn't just cheer when you win—but prays when you want to quit. You need people who celebrate your anointing and challenge your blind spots. The kind of people who don't just hype you up—but hold you up.

Also, recognize that support isn't just vertical (mentors)—it's horizontal (peers) and even generational (those you pour into). When you lead, you need others who lead. When you give, you need spaces to receive. It's a flow. It's a family. It's a *faith ecosystem.*

Invest in relationships that stretch you. Be intentional about community, even if it feels vulnerable. That could mean joining a faith-based mastermind, hiring a Kingdom coach, participating in a prayer circle, or finding a mentor who's *anointed and equipped.*

And here's the key: **your breakthrough is often connected to who you're walking with.** Don't let pride, perfectionism, or past hurt keep you isolated. *Your next level might be one conversation, one connection, or one collaboration away.*

Support System Action Steps:

1. **LIST YOUR CURRENT CIRCLE**
   Who's speaking into your life and business? Are they faith-fueled or fear-based?

2. **IDENTIFY GAPS**
   Do you need a mentor, coach, accountability partner, or prayer partner right now?

3. **TAKE ONE BOLD STEP**
   Reach out, join a group, or ask for prayer support. Don't isolate. Initiate.

SURROUND YOURSELF WITH FAITH-FUELED SUPPORT

Journal Prompts:

- Who has been a source of encouragement in my journey—and how can I honor that?

  _____
  _____
  _____
  _____

- Where have I allowed isolation to rob me of community?

  _____
  _____
  _____
  _____

- What kind of support do I need most in this season—and who might God be calling me to connect with?

  _____
  _____
  _____
  _____

KINGDOM KEY 09

Keep the Vision Before You

"Write the vision and make it plain... Though it linger, wait for it; it will certainly come and will not delay."

– HABAKKUK 2:2-3

The greatest threat to your calling is not failure—it's forgetting.

Forgetting what God said. Forgetting what He promised. Forgetting why you started.

When you lose sight of your vision, you lose steam, direction, and motivation. You start chasing distractions, comparing your progress,

KEEP THE VISION BEFORE YOU

or doubting your purpose. That's why Scripture says to **write the vision** — not just dream it, speak it, or post it... but *write it and make it plain.*

Why? Because vision leaks.
Because storms blur your view.
Because waiting can feel like wandering.

But when the vision is written down, it anchors you in seasons of delay, discouragements, and detours.

God isn't slow—He's strategic.

And sometimes what feels like a pause is actually **preparation**. That's why you must keep the vision **visible**—on your wall, in your journal, on your phone, in your planner—anywhere you can see it and pray over it.

Your vision is more than a business goal—it's a divine *blueprint.*

And the enemy's favorite strategy is **vision distortion.** He'll use fatigue, fear, financial pressure, and failed expectations to make you question if the vision was even real. But just because it's hard doesn't mean it's not holy.

When you don't keep the vision before you, **you'll start building based on circumstances instead of convictions.** That's how businesses drift, ministries dry up, and callings get buried under busyness. You must revisit what God originally said and stay connected to that assignment—even if you're in a temporary wilderness.

Every time you revisit your vision, your spirit gets recalibrated. What felt cloudy becomes clear. What felt heavy becomes light. Because when you remember the *why*, you regain strength for the *how*.

Vision is your compass. Without it, you'll chase trends, overwork yourself trying to prove something, or fall into the trap of imitation. But with vision? You can say "no" with confidence and "yes" with clarity. You move with purpose, not pressure.

Also—vision evolves. The seed stays the same, but the strategy can shift. Don't be afraid to adapt the **how** while staying anchored to the **why**. Let the Holy Spirit breathe fresh revelation into your vision as you grow in maturity and capacity.

Write it again. Read it again. Speak it again.
War with the vision when doubt creeps in.
Print it. Post it. Prophesy it.

Keep it so close that when lies try to speak, truth answers louder.

Your team, your clients, your community—they need you to hold the vision high. You are the steward of the assignment. If you let it fade, others miss out. You're not just building a business—you're building legacy, impact, and Kingdom culture. Keep that vision burning.

And finally, vision is not for vanity—it's for **victory.**
God gave you this vision not so you could b—but so you could **build.**

So build like you believe. Build like it's already blessed. Build like Heaven is backing you—because it is.

Vision Activation Steps:

① **WRITE OR REWRITE YOUR VISION**
Keep it short, Spirit-led, and clear.

② **POST IT WHERE YOU'LL SEE IT**
Include visuals, scriptures, and declarations that reinforce it.

③ **PRAY INTO IT WEEKLY**
Set aside intentional time to pray, declare, and ask for next steps related to the vision.

KEEP THE VISION BEFORE YOU

Journal Prompts:

🔒 When was the last time I revisited the vision God gave me?

_____
_____
_____
_____
_____

🔒 What distractions or doubts have clouded my focus?

_____
_____
_____
_____

🔒 How can I keep my vision visible, prayed over, and burning in this season?

_____
_____
_____
_____
_____

KINGDOM KEY 10

Align Your Schedule with God's Pace

"There is a time for everything, and a season for every activity under the heavens."

– ECCLESIASTES 3:1

You weren't created to run at the speed of social media. You were designed to move at the pace of grace.

Too many Kingdom entrepreneurs are building God-sized visions on *burnout-sized schedules*. But pressure does not equal progress. Pace matters. And if the pace of your life is choking your peace, draining your focus, and drowning out God's voice—it's time to reset your rhythm.

ALIGN YOUR SCHEDULE WITH GOD'S PACE

God has a pace for your purpose. A divine tempo. And when you sync your schedule with His Spirit, your days go from **chaotic to catalytic**. It's no longer about doing all the things—it's about doing *the right things at the right time, in the right season.*

The world screams "hustle."

But Heaven whispers "Holy Spirit, what now?"

That's the difference between worldly grind and Kingdom flow. When you allow God to lead your time, you don't just work harder—you work wiser. You learn when to sprint, when to rest, when to plant, and when to harvest.

When you align your time with God's pace, you shift from **productivity to purpose**. You're no longer filling your calendar to feel accomplished—you're filling it with intentional moves that reflect your assignment. This is where you stop reacting and start ruling your day.

Busyness isn't a badge of honor—it's often a symptom of misplaced priorities. Many entrepreneurs confuse movement with momentum. But you can be busy and still out of alignment. True Kingdom success is **peaceful, purposeful, and paced by grace.**

Let's be clear: rest is not laziness—it's obedience. God Himself rested on the seventh day. Jesus pulled away often to recharge. The Holy Spirit leads with peace, not pressure. When your life is overbooked, it's hard to hear Heaven. So take your schedule to the altar and ask: "God, **what's in this calendar that You never approved?**"

Sometimes alignment looks like *canceling a launch.* Sometimes it looks like *saying no to a good opportunity.* Sometimes it looks like *delaying something that's not time-sensitive so you can recover spiritually or emotionally.* When your pace is set by God, you're not just effective—you're in flow with favor.

Aligning your schedule also means building

ALIGN YOUR SCHEDULE WITH GOD'S PACE

margin—not just for meetings, but for **miracles.** Space for prayer. Time for divine interruptions. Room for rest, reflection, and relationships. You can't pour out well if you're running on empty.

If you want to thrive long-term, you need to protect your energy like it's sacred—because it is. Your schedule should reflect your *season*, your capacity, and your *assignment*. Stop comparing your pace to someone in a different season of life or business.

And here's the truth: God moves in **seasons**. What worked last quarter may not work this one. The clients you served before may shift. The offer that once grew your business may need refreshing. But when you align your planning and production to God's voice, you don't just *adapt*—you *advance*.

Also, don't forget to invite the Holy Spirit into your **weekly planning**. Let Him show you where to pause, what to prioritize, and how to pace your projects. He cares about your time—He's the Author of it.

When you align with His timing, doors open with ease. Clients find you without strain. Creative ideas flow. Stress decreases. Why? Because grace is flowing and *you're in sync* with Heaven's rhythm. You don't need to run harder—you need to run *with Him*. And sometimes, Kingdom pace means walking. Sometimes it means resting. But every time it means **trusting**.

Time Alignment Action Steps:

1. **DO A SCHEDULE AUDIT.**
   What's taking your time that God didn't assign you to?

2. **BUILD IN MARGIN**
   Create daily space for rest, prayer, and refreshment—even if just 15-30 minutes.

3. **HOLY SPIRIT PLANNING HOUR**
   Set time weekly to ask God, "What should I focus on this week?"

ALIGN YOUR SCHEDULE WITH GOD'S PACE

Journal Prompts:

Where have I been operating from pressure instead of peace?

_____
_____
_____
_____
_____

What would change if I truly aligned my pace with God's grace?

_____
_____
_____
_____

What rhythms bring me closer to clarity, creativity, and Christ?

_____
_____
_____
_____
_____

KINGDOM KEY 11

Use Feedback As Fuel

"Listen to advice and accept instruction, and in the end you will be wise."
– PROVERBS 19:20

Feedback isn't failure.
It's *fuel*—when you receive it with the right mindset and a Kingdom heart.

Many entrepreneurs avoid feedback because it triggers fear, insecurity, or perfectionism. But in the Kingdom, feedback is a gift. It's how God refines your delivery, sharpens your voice, strengthens your systems, and aligns your message with the people He's called you to reach.

USE FEEDBACK AS FUEL

You're not just **building a business**—you're becoming a vessel. And vessels get stretched. They get shaped. They go through the fire. That process often includes correction, critique, and insight that may not feel good—but will *grow* you.

The most anointed leaders are also the most teachable. David was a giant-slayer—but he still had a Nathan in his life. Paul wrote half the New Testament—but he still received correction and counsel. **If you want long-term fruit, you need short-term refinement.**

Avoiding feedback keeps you stuck at your current level. Receiving it with maturity moves you to your next one. Feedback reveals what's working, what's not, and what could be improved—not to shame you, but to **sharpen you.**

It's easy to become emotionally attached to your ideas, your branding, or your offers—but God is more concerned *about your effectiveness than your ego.* He will use feedback from clients, coaches, team members, and even critics to make you **more impactful and more aligned.**

And yes—some feedback will be messy. Unfair. Delivered poorly. But even in flawed delivery, God can use it for refinement. Don't throw away truth just because it came wrapped in discomfort. Mature leaders can extract wisdom even from wounded voices.

That said, you must **discern the source.** Not all feedback deserves a seat at the table. Some comes from fear, jealousy, or people who don't carry your assignment. Always weigh feedback against the Holy Spirit's voice, wise counsel, and your original calling.

One of the most powerful things you can do is ask for feedback *before* things fall apart. Ask your clients how you can serve them better. Ask your team what's unclear. Ask your audience what they're struggling with. This postures you as a **listener—not just a leader.**

USE FEEDBACK AS FUEL

And don't forget: feedback isn't just for correction—it's also confirmation. Sometimes God will use someone else's words to remind you you're on the right track. A client testimonial, a "that changed my life" message, or a repeat customer is **feedback from Heaven** that your obedience is working.

Train your spirit to filter feedback through faith, not fear. Instead of "I'm not good enough," you'll start hearing, *"This is helping me grow."* Instead of retreating, you'll refocus. Feedback doesn't push you backward—it pulls you **deeper into excellence.**

Feedback is also one of God's **tools for acceleration.** What would take years to learn on your own can be shifted in days through wise input. A small tweak in your messaging, a clearer process, or a better way to serve can lead to massive results—*if you're willing to listen.*

And finally, remember: this is Kingdom. You're not in this alone. Invite the Holy Spirit to help you **process, pray through, and implement** what you've received. Feedback in God's hands becomes *firepower*—not failure.

Feedback Activation Steps:

① **ASK FOR INSIGHT.**
Reach out to 3 clients, peers, or mentors and ask: "What's one area I could improve or clarify?"

② **PRAY THROUGH WHAT YOU RECEIVE**
Don't react—reflect and ask the Holy Spirit what applies to your season.

③ **REFINE ONE AREA THIS WEEK**
Choose one specific thing to adjust based on the feedback you've received.

USE FEEDBACK AS FUEL

Journal Prompts:

🔒 What feedback have I ignored, avoided, or feared—and why?

_____

_____

_____

_____

🔒 How can I develop a more teachable, humble heart?

_____

_____

_____

🔒 What is one area of my business or leadership that needs refinement right now?

_____

_____

_____

_____

KINGDOM KEY 12

Trust God With The Results

"Commit your works to the Lord, and your plans will be established."
– PROVERBS 16:3

You've planned. You've prayed. You've prepared.

You've built the offer, served the people, planted the seed.

Now—it's time to surrender the outcome.

True Kingdom success is not measured by sales or status; it's measured by **obedience.**

TRUST GOD WITH THE RESULTS

Many entrepreneurs say they trust God—until the launch underperforms, the client backs out, or the engagement tanks. Suddenly, doubt creeps in: *"Did I miss it? Was that even God?"*

But in Kingdom business, results aren't always immediate. Sometimes God is developing your **faith** before He multiplies your **fruit.**

He's not just producing results—He's shaping a *disciple.* Surrender is the ultimate strategy in Kingdom entrepreneurship. When you commit your work to the Lord, your heart moves from stress to rest. You become less focused on proving and more focused on *partnering* with God.

Trusting God with the results doesn't mean you stop showing up. It means you stop striving from a place of fear and start flowing from a place of faith. You continue to post, serve, pitch, and plan **—but with peace** as your posture. This is where excellence meets surrender, and grace leads the work.

Your greatest demonstration of faith isn't starting something—it's waiting well. It's continuing to show up when the numbers say no, but God still says go. God often works behind the scenes before He reveals things publicly. What feels like silence is often *strategy*.

While you're questioning your impact, God is preparing the stage. While you're doubting, Heaven is aligning. While you're waiting, **He's weaving purpose into your process.** There's no wasted obedience in the Kingdom.

Kingdom entrepreneurs must learn to measure results differently. Not by what you see, but by what you *sowed*. Obedience carries more weight than outcome. Legacy weighs more than likes.

Ask yourself: Did I serve with excellence?
Did I steward the idea God gave me?
Did I show up when it didn't make sense?
If yes—**you're already winning.**

TRUST GOD WITH THE RESULTS

Don't allow a slow season to distort your identity. God is not behind just because your numbers are. He's not delayed—He's **developing** you. And when the time is right, He will *elevate* you.

Trusting God with the results also means silencing the voice of comparison. Just because someone else is seeing faster growth doesn't mean you're behind. They're in their lane—and you're in yours. God's pace for you is *perfect*.

Celebrate others without doubting your direction. Honor what God is doing for them while staying rooted in your assignment. There's no shortage of success in the Kingdom. God's blessings are abundant—not limited.

When you trust God's timing, you release the need to rush. You stop worshiping the calendar and start walking in peace. You no longer ask, "How fast can I grow?" You begin to ask, "How deep can I go?"

Joseph had a vision—but he faced betrayal, false

accusation, and prison before the promise. His gift was real, but the process was painful. Even so, he remained faithful in the dark. And when the time came, **he was ready.**

The delay wasn't punishment—it was *positioning*. In that prison, Joseph's character was refined. His discernment deepened. His leadership matured.

That's what trusting the process looks like. And that's what trusting God with the results requires. Not blind optimism—but *bold surrender*. Not passive waiting—but *purposeful faithfulness*.

And when the breakthrough comes? Stay humble. Don't let success seduce you into self-reliance. Remember who brought the increase. Worship the *Source*, not the spotlight.

Real trust means staying as surrendered in promotion as you were in the process. It means continuing to seek God—not just the next opportunity. It means honoring the journey—

not just the results. This is spiritual maturity in motion.

Also—don't manipulate outcomes. Don't chase results by cutting corners or compromising truth. If you start something in the Spirit, you must sustain it by the Spirit. **Integrity is more important than influence.**

Kingdom results are birthed through obedience, not optimization. It's not about tricking algorithms or tweaking funnels—it's about trusting God. Be wise with strategy, but stay surrendered to the Spirit. Because what God initiates, He funds. What He speaks, He sustains.

Trust also looks like *celebrating before the harvest.* Faith praises *before* the doors open. It sows, serves, and shouts before the numbers show up. That's Kingdom confidence in action.

Say this with boldness: "I'm not waiting for results to believe—I believe, and so I'll see."

"I trust God not because of what I see, but because of who He is."
"I sow in obedience and leave the harvest in His hands."

This is your final key—but it's really the foundation. Everything you've built, written, launched, and led—**place it at His feet**. Lay your brand, your clients, your income, and your visibility on the altar. Say with full conviction: *"Lord, not my will, but Yours be done."*

Because at the end of the day, all the marketing, strategy, systems, and sales won't carry you like the *Spirit* will. If God isn't in it, the grind will exhaust you. But if God breathes on it, the growth will glorify Him. Trust Him. He is faithful. He is just. He is *good*.

TRUST GOD WITH THE RESULTS

Result-Release Action Steps:

1. **SOW + RELEASE**
   At the end of each launch or offer, say aloud: "God, I did my part. Now I trust You with the harvest."

2. **BREAK THE TIMELINE**
   Delete artificial deadlines rooted in fear. Replace them with faith-driven trust.

3. **CELEBRATE NOW**
   Write down 3 wins from your obedience—regardless of visible outcomes.

Journal Prompts:

What area of my business am I struggling to surrender?

_____
_____
_____
_____
_____

🔒 How have I been measuring success—and does it align with the Kingdom?

🔒 If I fully trusted God with the outcome, how would I show up differently?

Faith-based
Journal Prompts
&
Scriptures

FAITH-BASED JOURNAL PROMPTS & SCRIPTURES

Let the Word Be Your Blueprint.
Let the Spirit Be Your Strategy.

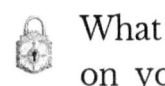
What specific business idea has God placed on your heart that you've been hesitant to pursue?

> *"Write the vision and make it plain."*
> – HABAKKUK 2:2-3

Describe a time when you allowed fear to pause your progress. What truth from God's Word cancels that fear?

> *"For God has not given us the spirit of fear, but of power, and of love, and of a sound mind."*
> – 2 TIMOTHY 1:7

FAITH-BASED JOURNAL PROMPTS & SCRIPTURES

 What does "doing business God's way" look like for you in this season?

> *"Commit to the Lord whatever you do,
> and he will establish your plans."*
> – PROVERBS 16:3

In what areas of your business do you feel confident? Where do you still need clarity or courage?

> *"Being confident of this, that he who began a good work in you will carry it on to completion."*
> – PHILIPPIANS 1:6

_____
_____
_____
_____
_____
_____
_____
_____
_____
_____
_____
_____
_____
_____

What scriptures ground your identity as a Kingdom entrepreneur?

> *"You are the light of the world. A city on a hill cannot be hidden."*
> – MATTHEW 5:14

_____
_____
_____
_____
_____
_____
_____
_____
_____
_____
_____
_____
_____
_____
_____
_____

Reflect on a moment when God provided a resource, connection, or opportunity that only He could orchestrate.

> *"And my God shall supply all your need according to His riches in glory."*
> – PHILIPPIANS 4:19

___
___
___
___
___
___
___
___
___
___
___
___
___
___
___

How do you define success—and is your definition aligned with Heaven's?

> *"What does it profit a man to gain the whole world and lose his soul?"*
> – MARK 8:36

Write a prayer of surrender over your business. Let it be raw, real, and rooted in trust.

> *"Trust in the Lord with all your heart and lean not on your own understanding."*
> – PROVERBS 3:5-6

FAITH-BASED JOURNAL PROMPTS & SCRIPTURES

 What boundaries do you need to set in order to protect your peace and purpose as a CEO?

> *"Above all else, guard your heart, for everything you do flows from it."*
> – PROVERBS 4:23

_____
_____
_____
_____
_____
_____
_____
_____
_____
_____
_____
_____
_____
_____
_____

Where have you been operating from hustle instead of grace? What does rest in obedience look like for you?

> *"Come to me, all you who are weary and burdened, and I will give you rest."*
> — MATTHEW 11:28

_____
_____
_____
_____
_____
_____
_____
_____
_____
_____
_____
_____
_____
_____
_____
_____

FAITH-BASED JOURNAL PROMPTS & SCRIPTURES

 What do you sense the Holy Spirit saying to you about your current business model or offer?

> *"My sheep listen to my voice; I know them, and they follow me."*
> — JOHN 10:27

List three miracles you're believing God for in your business. Stretch your faith.

> *"Now to Him who is able to do immeasurably more than all we ask or imagine..."*
> — EPHESIANS 3:20

What mindset lies have you agreed with that you now renounce in Jesus' name?

> *"Do not conform to the pattern of this world, but be transformed by the renewing of your mind."*
> — ROMANS 12:2

_____
_____
_____
_____
_____
_____
_____
_____
_____
_____
_____
_____
_____
_____
_____

Who are you called to serve in this season? Get specific about your Kingdom assignment.

> *"Each of you should use whatever gift you have received to serve others..."*
> — 1 PETER 4:10

_____

_____

_____

_____

_____

_____

_____

_____

_____

_____

_____

_____

_____

FAITH-BASED JOURNAL PROMPTS & SCRIPTURES

 What testimonies from your personal journey can become tools to empower your audience?

> *"They triumphed by the blood of the Lamb and by the word of their testimony."*
> — REVELATION 12:11

How will you integrate prayer and prophetic vision into your daily business operations?

> *"Pray without ceasing."*
> — 1 THESSALONIANS 5:17

Reflect on your current circle. Are they faith-filled collaborators or comfortable bystanders?

> *"Iron sharpens iron, so one person sharpens another."*
> — PROVERBS 27:17

_____
_____
_____
_____
_____
_____
_____
_____
_____
_____
_____
_____
_____
_____

What are you afraid of losing if you go all in on your calling?

> *"Whoever wants to save their life will lose it, but whoever loses their life for me will find it."*
> — MATTHEW 16:25

_____
_____
_____
_____
_____
_____
_____
_____
_____
_____
_____
_____
_____
_____

FAITH-BASED JOURNAL PROMPTS & SCRIPTURES

 What legacy are you building—and how will it glorify God beyond your lifetime?

> *"A good person leaves an inheritance for their children's children."*
> — PROVERBS 13:22

_____
_____
_____
_____
_____
_____
_____
_____
_____
_____
_____
_____
_____
_____
_____

Write your "I am" statement as a faith-driven entrepreneur. Declare it boldly.

> *"Let the redeemed of the Lord say so."*
> — PSALM 107:2

FAITH-BASED JOURNAL PROMPTS & SCRIPTURES

 What systems or habits must you develop to steward your next level?

> *"Whoever can be trusted with very little can also be trusted with much."*
> — LUKE 16:10

_____
_____
_____
_____
_____
_____
_____
_____
_____
_____
_____
_____
_____
_____
_____

When was the last time you celebrated progress, not perfection?

> *"Do not despise these small beginnings..."*
> — ZECHARIAH 4:10

How are you using your voice in the marketplace? Are you hiding, or heralding hope?

> *"Open your mouth for the mute, for the rights of all who are destitute."*
> — PROVERBS 31:8

Write a thank-you note to your future self for not giving up.

> *"Let us not grow weary in doing good, for in due season we will reap..."*
> — GALATIANS 6:9

_____
_____
_____
_____
_____
_____
_____
_____
_____
_____
_____
_____
_____
_____
_____

FAITH-BASED JOURNAL PROMPTS & SCRIPTURES

 What would it look like if you truly believed that God is your CEO?

> *"The Lord will guide you always; He will satisfy your needs..."*
> " — ISAIAH 58:11

___
___
___
___
___
___
___
___
___
___
___
___
___
___
___

Closing
Thoughts
& Next Steps

Closing Thoughts:
SEALED IN REFLECTION, POSITIONED FOR BREAKTHROUGH

My dear Kingdom trailblazer,

You've done something powerful. You've paused to reflect—not just with your mind, but with your spirit. And in that sacred space, healing happens. Clarity flows. Assignments activate. When we slow down long enough to listen, the Holy Spirit doesn't whisper—He *reveals*.

These journal prompts weren't just questions.

They were divine invitations—open doors to deeper alignment, fresh fire, and unshakable

CLOSING THOUGHTS:

faith. Whether you journaled in tears, praise, or stillness, know this: you are now further rooted, clearer in purpose, and more dangerous to the enemy than ever before.

Keep these reflections close. Revisit them often. God doesn't speak just once—He speaks in layers, in seasons, in waves. What He revealed today is only the beginning.

More is coming. Stay open. Stay obedient. Stay expectant.

And remember: You are Business & Blessed. Not because it's trendy—but because it's your truth. You were handpicked for this moment, appointed to lead in both purpose and profit, called to thrive in both spiritual and strategic realms.

Let the words you've written become war cries, vision maps, and fuel for your next move.

Now take a breath... and get ready for your next elevation.

With honor and expectation,

Dr. Renee Sunday, MD
Voice of Purpose | Midwife to Destiny | Marketplace Minister

Next Steps:
YOUR STRATEGY SESSION INVITATION

Let's Align, Activate, and Accelerate—Together

Beloved Visionary,

You've reflected. You've been poured into. Now it's time to take *strategic* and *Spirit-led* action.

I don't believe in coincidence—I believe in divine alignment. And if you've made it this far in *Business & Blessed*, then you're ready for more than just inspiration. You're ready for *activation*.

That's why I'm personally inviting you to book a **One-on-One Strategy Session** with me.

This isn't a cookie-cutter consultation. This is a purpose-driven, Holy Ghost-filled conversation that will help you:
- Clarify your business vision and spiritual mandate
- Pinpoint profit gaps and kingdom impact opportunities
- Identify the next steps to build, scale, or shift—without compromise
- Receive prophetic insight and practical strategy tailored to your calling

Whether you're launching, growing, or rebranding—this session will unlock momentum.
- Let's align your faith and your framework.
- Let's silence confusion and amplify clarity.
- Let's activate your next level—on purpose, in power

☑ Schedule Your Strategy Session Today

You're not meant to figure it all out alone. Let's build together—with excellence, with divine

NEXT STEPS: YOUR STRATEGY SESSION INVITATION

order, and with unstoppable faith.

This is your season of supernatural strategy and multiplied results.

Let's go!

In purpose and power,

Dr. Renee Sunday, MD
Kingdom Business Architect | Legacy Midwife | Your Faith-Driven Coach

STAY CONNECTED

Schedule Your Strategy Session Today:

About the
Author

ABOUT THE AUTHOR

About Dr. Renee Sunday, MD

The Kingdom and Legacy Builder

Dr. Renee Sunday, MD, is internationally recognized as The Kingdom and Legacy Builder—a prophetic voice, powerhouse mentor, and anointed business architect called to disrupt the marketplace for the glory of God.

A trailblazer in both medicine and ministry,

Dr. Renee transitioned from a successful career as an anesthesiologist to become a global force in faith-based entrepreneurship.

As an ordained minister, media personality, and CEO of multiple thriving brands—including Sunday Publishing and the Faithpreneur Academy—she has helped thousands of visionaries birth books, businesses, broadcasts, and movements rooted in both excellence and eternity.

Through her signature framework, Business & Blessed, she equips high-impact leaders to:

- Align their divine purpose with scalable profit
- Build legacy systems that outlast them
- Serve boldly in both the church and the boardroom

Dr. Renee is the host of the internationally streamed Good Deeds Radio & TV Show, a multi-time best-selling author, and an award-winning publisher. But beyond the platforms

ABOUT THE AUTHOR

and programs, she is a servant-leader devoted to healing hearts, igniting callings, and elevating Kingdom influence.

Her voice carries prophetic weight. Her strategies deliver measurable results. And her mission is urgent:

To raise up a generation of Kingdom CEOs who build legacies, break cycles, and blaze trails that Heaven celebrates.

CONNECT WITH DR. RENEE:

Connect with Dr. Renee:

🌐 DrReneeSunday.com

IG / FB / YouTube: @DrReneeSunday

Join the movement:
www.BusinessAndBlessedBook.com

Book her to speak, mentor, or host:
info@DrReneeSunday.com

Notes

Notes

Notes

Notes

Notes

Notes

Notes

Notes

Notes

Notes

Notes

Notes

Notes

www.ingramcontent.com/pod-product-compliance
Lightning Source LLC
Chambersburg PA
CBHW050912160426
43194CB00011B/2373